25 untold secrets of successful people

Introduction

What's the subtle strategy? Truly, it's anything but a simple inquiry to respond to. Be that as it may, many individuals have become fruitful by dominating a few key propensities.

How would they make it happen? Are there any insider facts that you have close to zero familiarity with?

In reality, indeed, there are!

In any case, when you know these mysteries, you'll understand that they are really direct. Achievement is difficult, yet it is fundamental, straightforward.

Thus, I dug further into the meetings, books, and accounts of these fruitful individuals to present to you a strong perception of what it resembles inside their brains.

Here, I present you, the propensities for fruitful individuals.

1. To impact the world, change yourself.

Jack Mama, the organizer behind Alibaba Gathering, recognized in a meeting: "It is the most critical to "Change ourselves."

To see yourself effective in decade from now, then you have to look yourself in the mirror and inquire "What is it that I believe should do consistently until the end of my life?"

Do that.

Compose a strong vision for your life since you have one life and there is not a great explanation to accomplish something you disdain. That additionally implies, quit your normal everyday employment at the earliest opportunity, on the off chance that you're distraught making it happen.

2. Quit being sluggish.

This must be the main propensity here. In Aaron Marino's words, "The mystery? Try not to fuck apathetic. That is the main mystery for you, me, everyone to find lasting success."

3. It's ideal to do one thing incredibly well.

Every single effective individual and organizations have this something significant normal: they pick a certain something and show improvement over every other person. That's what google trusts. Also, we understand what they're great at.

Work on everything. Try not to confuse things and be clear about what you can do best. Google began with the web search tool. After it was adequately extraordinary, items like Guides and Gmail were conceived.

You can be a handyman, yet all the same individually. Ace one craftsmanship, expertise or anything you can do best. Be awesome, to fabricate a vocation around it. Be great to the point that you'll be viewed as the best of all.

When you're adequate in doing one thing then invest energy

dominating something different. Having numerous abilities generally helps and occupies more space in your portfolio.

4. Quit pursuing the enchanted projectiles.

A youngster began his music vocation at four years old lastly got some notoriety at the age of 25. Presently, he goes by the name Bruno Mars.

It is not difficult to become involved with easy money scams and alternate routes. In any case, numerous business people don't figure out reality. Ramit Sethi concurred, "Whether you're attempting to begin a business, get a new line of work, or work on your wellness... Wizardry Projectiles DON'T EXIST."

Achievement doesn't come that quick, generally speaking. It requires a long time of difficult work and tolerance.

5. Try not to work for cash. Figure out how to bring in cash work for you.

"My recommendation to every one of you is, don't work for cash — it will break down quick, or you won't ever make enough and you won't ever be blissful, either," Tim Cook inferred.

Robert Kiyosaki rehashed a few times in his book: "work to learn, don't work for cash." When that's what you comprehend, you will get away from a futile way of life. In less difficult words, you'll not be bringing in cash for fellows in pants and tee shirts. Maybe figuring out how you have some control over the cash and making it work for you.

To see all the more obviously, read Rich Father, Unfortunate Father.

6. You haven't attempted an adequate number of times assuming that you wish to stop.

SpaceX bombed various times and lost large number of dollars until they at long last got the very first reusable rocket Bird of prey 9 to work.

"Disappointment is a choice here. On the off chance that things are not falling flat, you are not sufficiently advancing," said Elon Musk.

Anxiety toward disappointment is genuine. Disappointment isn't. In spite of the fact that it is an important stage on the way of progress, we have been molded attempting to stay away from it. They believe it's awful.

The achievement comes in the wake of flopping again and again, truth be told. In this way, in the event that you have a splendid business thought, begin testing and executing until you get it going. You got one life, don't bite the dust with laments.

At the point when a columnist inquired, "How could it feel to bomb multiple times?" Thomas Edison answered, "I didn't bomb multiple times. The light was an innovation with 1,000 stages."

7. Flawlessness isn't required.

Since we attempt such a great amount to not fizzle, many become fixated on idealizing everything. "Which blue will look the best? Dull blue or naval force blue? Ok, we should go with pink all things being equal."

Two things that I know to be valid:

Shown improvement over great.

Nothing is at any point awesome.

8. Quit watching others' victories on Instagram.

You're not taking a gander at the a long time of difficult work and battle, yet the gorgeous item that they are depicting themselves as. Quit having those superfluous transient highs. Since someone who might be listening is outpacing you, while you're twofold tapping pictures of Kardashians or Jenners.

9. Detach yourself from the rest of the world.

Nikola Tesla recommended:

"Most people are so caught up in the examination of the rest of the world that they are entirely careless in regards to what is passing on inside themselves. The psyche is more honed and quicker in disengagement and continuous isolation. No large research facility is required in which to think. Creativity flourishes in withdrawal liberated from outside impacts beating upon us to handicap the imaginative psyche. Be separated from everyone else, that is the mystery of creation; be distant from everyone else, that is when thoughts are conceived."

10. Battle what you love. Love what you battle.

"Delight in the gig invests flawlessness in the effort." - Aristotle

I'll take a few lines from Imprint Manson's success:

"What decides your prosperity isn't, "What is it that you need to appreciate?" The pertinent inquiry is, "What torment would you like to maintain?" The way to joy is a way brimming with shitheaps and disgrace. That is the hard inquiry that is important, the inquiry that will really get you some place."

All things considered, you want to battle something since that is where the significance of life comes from. Be that as it may, working at a call community, listening how somebody's crap got broke and attempting to fix it — this doesn't look fun by any stretch of the imagination, essentially to me.

At the point when gotten some information about his main goal to cultivate Mars, Elon Musk said: "I'm not saying we will make it happen, I'm saying we will attempt." all in all, he cherishes this battle.

What you do — expertise, workmanship or whatever — is your image. Fixate on your image. It characterizes you and your relationship with your client/prospect. This adoration for your work individuals will come to you in spite of many others offering a similar careful help.

11. Be proactive.

This is the main propensity that Stephen R. Flock discussed in his smash hit book. Being proactive can be made sense of in two places:

Try not to grumble and fault others.

Be reaction capable of the things you have some control over.

Life doesn't simply occur. It's a consequence of your decisions. Perceiving that and being responsible for those decisions — is being proactive. Responding to or agonizing over the outer powers and accusing others, which you have almost no control — isn't.

12. Continue to thump on entryways.

In the event that you're a novice, don't quit requesting guidance and moving toward influential individuals until somebody says OK. Numerous fledglings stress what others will think and so forth.

The truth of the matter is, I've met such countless persuasive individuals who are prepared to help (when moved toward the correct way). To such an extent that, I got 44 fruitful business people to contribute for my post about administration characteristics. I never knew until I began investing some energy.

Find individuals who have done something you need to do. Visit them or take them to lunch, and ask them for tips and deceives. They'll joyfully share since they're energetic about it.

13. Perusing consistently is one normal propensity for super fruitful individuals.

14. Study constantly the greats.

Rodney Jerkins expressed this about Michael Jackson while going for the XSCAPE narrative:

"Michael would be in a parlor watching film of Jackie Wilson, James Brown and Charlie Chaplin. Furthermore, he was about likely forty when we were cooperating. I stroll in and I say

"What are you doing?" He said, "I'm examining." Remind you, he had all the Grammys, a great many collections sold, I said, "What are you contemplating?" He said, "You study constantly the greats." That was a significant, serious example so that me as a youthful and forthcoming individual could hear him say that and to observe that."

15. Continuously do the statistical surveying.

Test. Test. Test.

It is so significant in light of the fact that it assists you with telling key business questions. Who will purchase your item? How frequently will individuals yet it? What amount would it be advisable for it to cost? And your rivals?

Above all: Do individuals truly require it? Will it make their life more straightforward/better? It may not be guaranteed to take care of a consuming issue, however ought to be sufficient.

The arrangement is, understanding the market is a constant interaction. Patterns, interests, contest, and so forth, change constantly, so should your system, objectives, and vision.

16. Be strong and unconventional.

This is what Felix Kjellberg (otherwise known as PewDiePie) said in one of his recordings (in the event that you don't have the foggiest idea, he's one of the most sought after persons on YouTube):

"In the event that I notice a channel accomplishing something I haven't seen previously, I'm consequently more attracted to that thing. Also, it was exactly the same thing for me when I began making recordings, I did what every other person was doing. Yet, my channel didn't develop from it by any stretch of the imagination. The large ones have previously gotten comfortable. It will be hard as damnation. Also, it was only after I begun doing unique, something that hadn't been finished previously, similar to the frightfulness recordings. That is the point at which I began to get a crowd of people that truly thought often about the substance that I was making."

Make a propensity for finding and accomplishing something that will assist you with isolating from the group. It very well may be whatever invigorates individuals. In any case, don't be so expect-capable and self-evident.

17. Never report your next enormous move.

Since when you do, individuals will give you assessments which generally have no worth. Those suppositions will divert you from your objectives and thusly, make you less roused to achieve them.

Companions, family members, or colleagues, they in all

probability won't figure out, criticize your arrangements and say: "This won't work, kid!" "Find a genuine line of work."

Set up your brain against all negative and putting impacts down. Numerous world-changing thoughts are conceived and dissipated in a matter of moments due to the feeling of dread toward analysis.

"You can't make it happen." "The occupation is too large."

"What will your family members think about you?"

Try not to allow them to stop you, at any expense. I believe it's a hot spot to utilize that famous statement: "Really buckle down peacefully, let your prosperity be your clamor."

18. Think shared benefit.

If you have any desire to find actual success, you can't be just contemplating yourself. This isn't about who wins and loses. Maybe looking for common advantage or answers for everybody.

Think mutual benefit implies everyone wins. Not just you bring in cash, everyone does.

19. Encircle yourself with fruitful individuals or the people who are en route to become effective.

One thing I might want to add is, find true success yourself or while heading to becoming one. Since you can't be passing judgment on individuals in the event that you're a failure.

20. Get the best to work for you.

Recruiting more individuals or not is altogether dependent upon you.

Be that as it may, you can't maintain a business independently assuming you maintain that it should become greater. That is the reason getting extraordinary representatives is essential and one of the most troublesome positions when your point is to extend.

Get more intelligent and more productive individuals than you. You need the most ideal ability. Since compromising with half-great isn't a choice.

In the event that you're an independent business visionary, bringing in sufficient cash and have a satisfied outlook on the thing you're doing then may not require more representatives. In any case, keep yourself presented to truly shrewd individuals and extraordinary information sources.

21. Quit purchasing stuff you needn't bother with.

Since you likely needn't bother with the stuff you figure you do.

It's perfect to purchase new and costly things while you're bringing in cash. Yet, a large number of us gain out of influence in any event, when it's of next to zero use.

How much stuff do you really want? That really relies upon your way of life and family.

What I know without a doubt, satisfaction doesn't come from claiming assets, yet educational encounters when experienced with others. Disposing of that stuff make you more joyful and your life simpler.

Keep in mind, you become rich by claiming huge load of cash, not by burning through large chunk of change. Here's the reason the following propensity is so significant.

22. Construct resources and lessen liabilities.

Above all else, what's a resource?

In straightforward words, a resource is something you own that assists you with bringing in cash, straightforwardly or in a roundabout way (like stocks and land). On the off chance that it's sucking your cash as opposed to making, it's a responsibility (like home credits).

Building resources, for the most part through stocks made Bill Doors and Warren Smorgasbord the most extravagant men on earth.

Like I said before, keep more cash than you spend. Before you can construct resources, figure out how to do that and be great at it. Robert T. Kiyosaki said, "The absolute most remarkable resource we as a whole have is our brain. In the event that it is prepared well, it can make gigantic abundance."

23. Work out and eat great food.

Your business can be spot on, and your connections can be on the money yet what might be said about your wellbeing?

To get huge things done you need to make a major stride towards your wellbeing and wellness. There is no hanging tight for New Year or birthday, roll out the psychological improvement now and begin working out.

Be responsible to yourself or recruit a wellness/wellbeing mentor.

The principal reason is to feel far better, over the long haul, not for a brief time frame. You'll be more athletic, more productive and in any event, when you'll be 60 or 90 years of age — you will be in a vastly improved position than if you keep away from it.

What's more, obviously, this won't be simple. For what reason would it be a good idea for it to be? There is in every case a cost to pay, and it will require investment.

24. Be energetic about your connections and sexual coexistence.

Napoleon Slope said in his hit:

"Sex change is straightforward and handily made sense of. It implies the exchanging of the brain from contemplations of actual articulation, to considerations of another nature. The longing for sexual articulation is by a wide margin the most grounded and generally prompting of the relative multitude of human feelings, and for this very reason this craving, when tackled and changed right into it, other than that of actual articulation, may raise one to the situation with a virtuoso."

"When driven by this craving, men foster astuteness of creative mind, boldness, determination, diligence, and innovative capacity obscure to them at different times. So solid and affecting is the longing for sexual contact that men openly risk life and notoriety to humor it."

25. Be exceptionally quick.

As Gary Vaynerchuk said, "Speed is 4 billion times more significant than flawlessness."

Agonizing and thoroughly considering others' thought process of you is something contrary to speed. The most serious issue is that individuals need to fabricate their organizations to find lasting success in the span of a year, however their everyday execution speed is slow.

Speed is the right combination of tolerance and difficult work.

You're patient in the long haul and buckling down with speed consistently. Stop babbling considerations over the table, begin testing and investing them in energy. That is the way you'll be aware in the event that you can get it going.

Furthermore, one thing while I end this post: recollect, not the propensities I've talked about are all vital. Some are, others not.

Additionally, I realize I haven't covered this theme altogether. I thought, how about we compose the main propensities

I've sorted out and afterward see what you have in your arms stockpile. Inform me and every other person as to whether you know an extraordinary propensity that is helping/assisted you with finding true success.

www.ingramcontent.com/pod-product-compliance
Lightning Source LLC
Chambersburg PA
CBHW071143220526
45467CB00015B/1783